I Want to Be Your Radio

by Sheila E. Murphy

Unlikely Books
www.UnlikelyStories.org
New Orleans, Louisiana

Unlikely Books
www.UnlikelyStories.org
New Orleans, Louisiana

I Want to Be Your Radio

In loving memory of Beverly A. Carver

1934 - 2022

Contents

I. how many butterflies
The Moment ... 13
You Music Me ... 14
Repertoire ... 15
Long Live Present Tense ... 16
I Want to Be Your Radio ... 18
A Field of Femininity ... 19
You Know Me ... 20
from Lauds (37) ... 21
from Inaudible Ghazals (3) ... 22
The Woodwind Sphere above Middle C ... 23
Monsoon Pantoum ... 24
Walk the Sweet Walk ... 26
On the Dance ... 27
Hand Pay ... 28
Last Call ... 29
Before ... 30
Oh Tapestry, the Inverse of an Innocence ... 31

II. key lime choreography
Early June ... 35
Shaping ... 36
Then ... 37
(In)audible Ghazals ... 38
The Prodigal Son Returns Home to the Empty Nest ... 40
Status Quo ... 41
Lust to Rust ... 42

Small Consolation 43
Singularities 44
French Horn 46
Spring Ghazal 47
"the only eulogy" 48
Three Ghazals 49
Narration 52
abecedarian 53
Six Nouns in Search of a Verb 54
In Celebration of Mistakes 56
The Ping of Code Words 57
For Jessica Smith 58
Stet Fret 60
Uninterrupted Screen Time 62
As Seen 63
Seashells in the Seychelles 64
Seen On Screen 65

III. whose guests we always are
It Is Trying to Fail to be a Monument 69
"Extrasensory emancipation yields to" 70
Four Autumn Ghazals 71
My Sole Excuse 75
Three Poems 76
No Gravity 82
14 Observations 83
A Saturday 86
Ashwagandha 87
A little Somersault 89

Everything I Did   90
Today   91
The Rain   92
White Statue   93
You Erased Penury and Wrote my Heart   95
Spring   96

Acknowledgments   99
About the Author   100
Other Books by Sheila E. Murphy   101
Recent Titles from Unlikely Books   104

I

how many butterflies

The Moment

Take this
punctuation, drive
through nightfall.

Flood me twice
more than my
mantra.

Dosages run
deep.
I invent you

in my free time,
free rein, free
zone.

Come see.

You Music Me

It is the harvest, the residue of objects
that in and of themselves will sing
when touched

I hear trees sloughing off the rigid coats around them
I listen to smooth bark beneath
always letting go

The symphony (You music me)
is peace is new is sweet
I am the evidence

of your everlast your smile
your song the derivations
of contagious knowing I seek

Repertoire

Her light, the fidgety arrangement of things in view for her. A numb floss trails across the table post use. Routine a given amid moderato morning. Deflected shock waves equivalent to past tense. Now light vigor of leftovers in the mind placed here and here. A dove, its gray breast no longer visible. The tone once settling. Infinite lines to hinge one noticed moment to the next. They each break down, now an array of listless infancies, a legacy.

Pinch hitter, unfamiliar in the territory, a trill of contribution

Long Live Present Tense

Her shimmering vocabulary mists through recollected hearing
As Schubert's Impromptu plays its contrast
Of insistent melody between flourishes of treble tones
She speaks to imaginary beings resting on her table
I nod and appreciate this pale echo of her being
A genius mild in mind now small as her thin bones

The softness of our flesh covers the insistent bones
We live defined by the constant sense of hearing
Each touch point, a synecdoche for being
I hear her speech and sense insistent contrast
As shared life comes down to this small table
Blessed by her still treble flourishes in tones

Variation on the tacit magic of familiar tones
Imaginary playthings rise from the premises leaving bones
A smooth dark surface defines the flat table
My way thinking reveals the constant hearing
A blend of old and now replete with contrast
That captures life in this once strong being

I like to think of purity as ageless being
She sings favorite songs in shapely chorded tones
The little world now left is plump with contrast
Any day now there will surface the reality of bones
I trust the closely held sense of hearing
Resembling ideas long debated before getting on the table

How is it possible to understand the simplicity of a table?
We claim to recognize our many selves as evidence of being
When she sings, I stop everything to invest in hearing
Each of her precisely formed clear and velvet tones
I recognize her beauty in the quiet sturdy bones
Letting go past moments in vivid contrast

How does feeling guide us to startling contrast?
All we own, placed safely or unsafely on a tiny table
We speak of basics that we know and call them bones
Every moment of our sensibility is perceived as being
As the mockingbird releases pretty tones
That release arpeggios within hearing

Long live present tense within our hearing
Each a sterling moment of delicious tones
Brushing against contrast on the table of our being

I Want to Be Your Radio

This dis-
cursive urge
to open up and
sing tetrameter
in praise of leggy
and continually
permanent zest
I fasten on
means sound forever
in the psyche patched
to last beneath these
heavenly opinionated
yawlings prepped
to host the feast
not fail the forward
ing but match
the hatching of yet more
trebling possibilities
to snatch daylight
from calm otherwise
and meander as a soul
into the sure reality
of all of us robust
when joined thus
in robusto gusto
of the constant
midnight song
across a constant highway

A Field of Femininity

Let me in on a little secret that I promise not to tell you. It is winter in my heart. At midnight, pockmarks on the floor above me fill with oxygen. Staccato heels (I do not mean stiletto) snap the ice I would prefer to keep in one piece. Projected early flowers turn medallions. I mean precision metal to salute. Scars you cannot see upon my ceiling change the stasis I desire. Complicit gestures spark agreement we don't reify. Abstraction means a constancy of sensibility, of breeding. Meanwhile in Tasmania, ribbons of lavender form a field of femininity. We practice Haydn on the early instruments. If only to incite a reciprocity in listening.

You Know Me

You know me and my infallible mistakes
The angel of spheres chastens legacy as mere mention
I prefer harmonics to full throated tones
If you love me (when) whisk something away that surfaces may be
        clean

You know me and my Constantinople focus
Long may ideas thrive amid threats and interruptions
The sacrament of busy-ness will always interfere with meaning
Make a note of whimsy while you work your way away

You know me and my spare plane of vision just across the room
Where flowers thrived now lives a polished surface appointed with
        chrome things
Function lives across where I can't see it
To the right of emptiness, framed moments of diploma linger

You know me and my makeshift diplomacy
The walls between us twerk impulsively apart from catechism
In my spare time I round up mental models and I fire them
Transition tingling vaults across what we once shared holds still for
        once

from **Lauds (37)**

Diagram eternity by fondling voice prints
Deck the diamantes, press the flesh
of artichokes and you and spun shine
all across the pieced yard
where gamecocks skitter
and the weeds are still too beautiful
to chip or pluck.

The quagmire that is reason softens
ease apres the bonny nest,
while berries transpose benignity
where no one sight-sees.
Instead, the glaze above rosacea
blooms fact of the matter
homespun lockstep adages
we norm to in our nether sleep.

from **Inaudible Ghazals**

3/

Nights she does not drink, she lives through, watching television,
talks about the drinking times before, the times to come.

A child stands at the frosted window, looking at the many
things to count, too many to begin, so takes in color, shapes.

Words happen by accident, life may not be chosen, but occurs
before being gathered up and spoken of, as though invented.

Framed mirror shows another side, retrieves what others see
and calls it something reductive, but a name.

What has grown is quiet now, the yard, on hiatus.
One can look there and forget occasions, all the dates, and times.

The Woodwind Sphere above Middle C

"Come Back to Sorrento" in a lime lit costume made of silk, and I will brine experience to taste. We need each altar we locate among the tiny fictions premised by each leisure rinse. With seaside bliss keepsakes in mind. The scape and silhouette of choice remands each fingering from thought. The composition shows its blessings and recedes as waves perform their tendencies. Refraction may repurpose the emotion welled beyond tepidity. Being equates to silvering along the precipice of midnight. Where gulls gather unseen astride presumptive light.

Monsoon Pantoum

So soft so safe to be within this home.
Humidity begins to empty onto rooftops.
I whisper over tea too hot to drink.
The shelf life of affection fades with breath.

Humidity begins to empty onto rooftops.
Dots of rain reach pavement.
The shelf life of affection fades with breath.
I look for photographs of moments I've deemed real.

Dots of rain reach pavement.
A wavy wind pushes across the span of lives.
I look for photographs of moments I've deemed real.
You are leaving and not coming back.

A wavy wind pushes across the span of lives.
Mourning brings no sweetness.
You are leaving and not coming back.
I age a little while then hold.

Mourning brings no sweetness.
Grief remains unpainted.
I age a little while then hold.
Memory reaches back to find vibrato.

Grief remains unpainted.
You appear in peace to all my senses.
Memory reaches back to find vibrato,
As storm approaches my pale heart.

You appear in peace to all my senses.
A minuet of daylight thins beneath this gray.
As storm approaches my pale heart,
Here within these rooms I finger melody.

A minuet of daylight thins beneath this gray.
I whisper over tea too hot to drink.
Here within these rooms I finger melody.
So soft so safe to be within this home.

Walk the Sweet Walk

Walk the sweet walk
after conversation dry the hands
as midnight cools the premises
we lark the brook light

and the summer senators go lithe
to reason pictures losing frames
we lie awake recalling
how a puzzle piece once missed

adjusts the landscape to mean
nothing flows again
and all the water heard
required a little wind

a breath at least
to move attention past
the lines of code
the watchful pasture of ascension

On the Dance

Some Mildred in our choreography keeps me awake, without reviving.
Offer me a sentence via lasso, and I'll reach. I'm quoting Jeremy
on the dance: "Run, run, leap, leap, emote, emote, emote." I know
Kathryn's looking down and laughing at the temperature deliciously
on par with wit. How many decibels does it take to form ballet that
lives within the mind throughout our destiny? If you can aim, you can
arrive. Integrity's the same as little symphonies striated into more
dimensions than one thought. A miniature becomes enormous just
as linearity transforms into what any monk can see with eyes closed
letting go of enmity as though a bubble of soft soap. A roundelay
intact remaining far above the fray.

Hand Pay

We can dream as we partake in games

to compensate for years of pain.

A gentle stretch away from what was vivid as a crossroads

showing two dismal realities.

Any way you cut it, there's a back room, likely dark,

with something to be signed

before you waltz away with pockets full of softness.

Un-cloistered places offer a way to hide and laugh

into the muffled space as private as a womb.

Largesse exceeding reciprocity

provides a cruising altitude for the duration.

Last Call

Her radio across the room leaks a single channel

featuring the music of deceased composers deemed valid at last.

She sees the sparkly ball of silver blue and rose dangling from the
ceiling fan and showing in the mirror just across from home plate bed.

Everything that happens is a sudden painting.

The numbers on the large digital clock straight ahead are news.

Each number has a language she delivers.

Whether anyone is there she lectures as she always did.

Clarifying, with inflection, bracing for her next responsibility.

Before

Before the rubble showed the building for what it had been, we left the windows open like invitations to the butterflies and birds and light wind. Before the harshness came a string of sweet soft words that lasted decades to the point that we knew no better than to expect them. Before the lampshade left the head and was placed out for bulk trash pickup, the light had been soft, romantic, and miraculous. Before the white elephant of a neighbor arrived at the gate, we were a happy family, large enough to feel protected. Before the exclamation points all died, we listened to the lilt of conversation flow across the lawns as manicured as sculpted snow. Before the chill arrived, we held the comfort of our skin and met each night with comfort, and as we dreamed we knew eternity as we imagined it would last.

Oh Tapestry, the Inverse of an Innocence

Plush intentional precision masks the underplay of taut weft threads.
How many butterflies have ripened in perception toward a story's
fragile strength? Not solely millefleur, the mind distinguishes backstory
from the foreground. Syllables infract the early teaching each may
disremember. Chanticleer comes home to roost, as all remain mere
integers.

Modus op, the blemishes of sport, impending string of rejoinders

II

key lime choreography

Early June

Key lime choreography
crimps elan along the parquet
with fleet footing newly
cogent for the nonce.

In parallel, quiescent fingerings
confide the story melody conveys
in piquant ways despite numbing ploys
that would capsize the dance.

Immune to beatific trance,
princes hover to acquire more land,
demand more power,
compounding their de facto gravity,

keeping them in traction
destined to return
to the recycling of chance
versus embracing the advance.

Shaping

Parse something do it for me
report back your loaded results
break down what you have found
in three short phrases
say a haiku
of separate laces

I will leave you
to consider our shared fate
if what you say longhand
and shorthand is true
do you believe in the power
of language to shape

how the world will be and if so
do you believe yourself
when you unload fractions of fact
and persuade as you are wont to do
do you believe in me
for believing in what you

contain explain entrain for surely
someone is headed somewhere
in full regalia or basic duds
about to appear somewhere else
amid something else to transform
what reality might mean or be or seem

Then

Long unplanned morning distorts the tipping point of fact. A yellow
tone upon the otherwise clear glass when storms appear olfactory.
A nimble mood that spawns regression to the mean. Some weeds
across the yard infringe upon intent. *I take back what I failed to say.*
Placeholder in thought guides toward impending darkness.

Fractions joined at random replicate dreamed sense of the whole

(In)audible Ghazals

1/

I write letters to his mind that loves looking
at the bricks from inside where the heater lives.

Champagne amounts to tincture, tidy looking
postcards take back innocence and fold it.

In a moment, sadness (its epitome) erupts
where I can grasp it, share, have it removed.

Pronouns recur as short cuts to truth
that stays truth bereft of usual music.

I was reared on woodwinds, those infinitely
high-maintenance reeds to fit oboes from France.

2/

I get a missive from across the sea: no e-
mail anymore, we're back to handmade letters.

Take the noise out of my ear and learn to blend
while there's still time: find pinball in these confines.

Puzzling is a word, and he keeps being that.
I pantomime; he shrugs off intonation.

Guy on bugle duty dazzles those on outdoor chairs
with brass sans valves, no plumbing, just tunes.

The soul won't zero out the only sin: unkindness,
according to the one who birthed me.

The Prodigal Son Returns Home to the Empty Nest

His mother who has not slept may now rest. Still in daylight she recites his name with all the meaning she can bring to the pair of tiny equal syllables. When she speaks that sound, a constellation of small points comes home to roost. Why did he leave, why has he put himself in debt, how come he never falls in love, what does he mean she did not love him in his youth? How to fix perception as the ground beneath is always shifting. Her fears have taken on a personality, and she pretends away the legacy without regard to who brought it to life.

Status Quo

All morning he delayed the afternoon. He used the word "confused"
to keep from working. Solicited opinions that might slow production.
He summarized what seemed wrong, inviting answers that he splayed
into new questions to preclude advancing tasks. Meanwhile, assorted
blooms convened in the far yard, a distance from the marigolds framed
by a near window. He thought of watering and mulching another
section of the yard that might provide a little light.

Pastime, duty, leisure melded into moments

Lust to Rust

His paramour is a white elephant.

Drives a macho vehicle and struts,

makes him seem feminine, despite his husky look.

The more he knows of her, the less

he wants to be alive in the small town

where people whisper how she ought to be

removed. He wanted someone

beautiful, exotic even, not this

ghost of drama, feeding on others' attention.

As the light diminishes, his body feels autumnal now.

Lost to an imagined history.

He dreams of growing back a personality.

Small Consolation

They sat muted in their separate rectangles looking identically forward.
The agenda was a theme and variations honoring the leader who could
afford straight teeth but kept the mildly crooked ones as if reminding
all that it was he who set the standard. Lots of jocular self-conscious
tittering failed to hide the shared embarrassment of being there.
Inclusion was a word; diversity, a label; equity, a dream. The prize of
being part of something, small consolation.

Singularities

We each in
our little cabinets
enclosed just navigate

the meeting of
some other cabinets
nudging about worlds

barely seen as
we push and
pull and hold

in still shots
strung together toward
a fluid picture

dramatized from within
played out from
without and storied

with bland dispatch
yet somehow sizzling
across the minds

that hitch to
speech and treble
to a pitch

unignorable just as
a thready excited
shrill young sounding

middle level one
persuades the self
of false energy

toward hoped contagion
nonetheless stability comes
and stays and

seeks beyond itself
some dazzle to
replace the rain

French Horn

The mouthpiece matched her modesty.

You could feel her meld of confidence with hesitation

as she pressed the tiny metal to her lips

to form a tone as mellow as a faun.

Her hand held the bell that shone in pale sunlight.

She kissed the notes that swirled together,

leaving legato pleasure in the room.

A music innocent as her young hands

lingered as she tucked the warm brass tubing

into the blue velvet case and closed the latch.

Spring Ghazal

Triple teeth convey the rapture in a comma
when a gnarl is frank as geometric volley.

Sink into my chair and parrot something streamlined,
that I may correct your grammar, free you from this house.

My auditory anguish rips open the sliding glass
downtime framed as minuet of splotchy steel.

Before I kiss away this frolic, let me season you.
I speak only with my turntable accompanied by eyes.

Everybody's sad to be in love today, and
as it happens there will be no roundelay.

The only eulogy
is singing
without sound

Three Ghazals

1/

World premiere of his icy composition on triangle
revealed the tonsure of neglect that brought him curbside.

A vintner knows his grapes, one would surmise, and thereby
fastens visual attention on a gustatory reminiscence.

In the food court of diminishing returns, the planet mercury
performs a moon walk for the mirror gentling our way forward.

Monastic orders comprehend the interweaving of
some integers, selected crayons, and a canvas.

An idea man who codified emotion
left his collection of clothespins to the docents.

2/

Imitation personalities go fast on auction sites.
To gather hand-weighed strings of pearls to match takes time.

Paternity differs from fatherhood in much the same way
that mimesis stays estranged from sacraments, with little to discuss.

At the lip of freedom is a story on the news of discerning
members of a growing audience who want to craft relationships.

In a room with windows dark there are no seasons to assume.
One selects not quite at random from among experiences.

Early in the class, the teacher assigned us to write on
"How it feels to be alive," but I was still young and conceptual.

3/

Five-thirty a.m. prettifies the landscape blotted otherwise with heat.
The household gallery holds feature photography of snorkels.

He gave me up for Lent, ahead of my intended venture to New
        Orleans.
That was before the, you know, and before the other thing you've read
        about.

Jazz ministers get rough with lay-by congregations who speak laissez-
        faire all day.
Show me a filament of mercy sometime when the wood smell is as
        good as tunes.

Crafts kicked the bucket list in elementary my dear grade school, the
        board
feathered underparts of desks and swivel chairs and dusted rungs of
        book space.

Lamentations rinse the thought that someone once deserved
        something that no one
ever earned the way a moment is received and held like a caesura on
        the page.

Narration

She store homes every oligarch she fails to see through thin light. Having read the drill espoused by noise mavens, she sylphs along imaginary roadways laced with ivy and perhaps a hypothetical porch. Rubs elbows with a hint of frost. Trespasses on edges each approaching frames as inventory sprawls across her screen of mind. Tastes gentleness as sweet young stilts guide forward.

A soliloquy, some depth perception, tacit tree line

abecedarian

anthropology is not my major
but has evolved to draw me
close by quiz prep to the
downside of experience as
elevation, shaping shorthand
fractals at first flea-sized then scaled
gargantuan before summer
heat expands to lay low toward
immediate centering that precludes
jaywalking as trespass on
kaleidoscopic umbrage taken
literally while drained of
meaning as midlife Maltese pet
named after the instructor
Quentin sparking various
rambunctious attitudes and
sleight of hand invasive as the
tacit grab for all thirty pieces of silver
under the cracking leaves with
voracious appetite propelling
walls of wannabe that once
x-rayed reveal shortcomings
you'd never a priori know as
zeal infusing daily life with greed.

Six Nouns in Search of a Verb

1/ Stalk

He gambled. The inevitable karma came to pounce when least
expected. Early morning flecks of light turned potent as a ladder was
repealed.

2/ Aspartame

Truss the wings to leave behind their span, form envy to erase. Is it
always winter here? Refinement seems part slave, part ladder. In a
shoelace moment, spine stays central as we brave the collar.

3/ Muse

Elbows her way into your modern (th)ought. Proves myth to be
derivative. You disbelieve source code as clatter. Noting marvels elapse
sans anyone along.

4/ Truck

He wants a pick(me)up, not this chipped paint sprawl of scarred bed
empty. Wait for a hypotenuse in depth-lined blue.

5/ Lessons

Failing to vocalize, term limits start to glow. A woven set of patches
once. And now bowed rain elapses as though . . .

6/ Caprice

Arrows out of wind long for the nonce. So smitten, she, dance-worthy, slim. What next, capitulation, maybe haptics. Maybe sloe gin fizz not gluten free merely the merry notes of reeds.

In Celebration of Mistakes

This continent that is my life includes bumps, ridges, and smooth places seen from mountaintops and little hills. A line of code precedes the rain. Lime green light affords a way of seeing branches and stems. I hold still, I reach, and learn to sing. I live the lake, the stream, prepare to find a road that breaks the sun. My feet are warm, the clothes once on the line I hold to me.

Sentences, a sentence within language not yet meant

The Ping of Code Words

Ungentle campaign speech exhaled into the bulbous head of
microphone. Why so thin a crowd? Anxiety about the look of weeds
beside the stands. Refraction of adulthood by way of repetition. Speech
planed across the surface to convey an imprimatur. *The fossil has
nodded.* Obsequious barbs conveyed the requisite nodding. Inelastic
prodding of a notion made to seem belief.

Crushed cellophane, a holding pattern, ephemeral white speech

For Jessica Smith

If   gentle

    soma

earthen flecks of joy

    (less or more legitimate

    (intimate

    (fresh

    Does each will to be

simplexity

    the naught pierce-penetrate

      ((eros dis

        integrates))

    As cloth loathe

    to gather close exceptions

a list

of quelled

dis)covered

pains(taking

odometers marking

Wisconsin or

anywhere

dye held

in cloth

change

quasi

(not speed skater not swimmer not editor)   de(fines

Do I read   half bifurcation

          voicing back or quieting to text that harbors while

re

          leasing   habitat

beneath between beyond r)each   uniceptual

parenthetical jarring and sweet center young   fore)cast

(may it last may it not   this

be lost may flowers   chi

reel in who we are   to

     if possible apart   fill

Stet Fret

Semitonic windmill slices
patch of air
on a G

string strung strummed
faultlessly (whee) watch
how nimble thimbles

spaced in rows
are (period) just
larking between firm

frets squared and
cubed into millions
sprawled on out

into strapless seeds
that lead to
weeding garden after

garden slowed and
gone unfertilized in
tandem with buoyant

thrive of look
alive you need
to be admired

you look in
on being looked
in on until

some tiny stranger
tugs your sleeve
it's you ago

en route halfway
to invented inverted
and shared destinations

Uninterrupted Screen Time

Which is heaven: a bespoke bot assigned to curb your enthusiasm
or uncensored free play leading to incessant fixation on the lingua
franca of hypotheses? *Snap out of it!* The proxy doll dovetails with the
delicately fresh face you winnowed from the culture as you framed
it: peachy little mood of resuscitated inference, let's say. Who needs
authority by a self-appointed clown with cobbled cred? How is leisure
different from lesions and ingrained poverty of heart?

As Seen

It's all so mostly in
appropriate you see
the gold around
the lettering intended
to be seen like starlets
standing by the pool

obsessing over what
he failed to say so busily
enmeshed in the discovery
of a structure over which
he would be king malingering
like some cheap imitation

of a shot approaching big
that winds up
shutting off somebody's life
before lifting off the ground
the sound the heart makes
cut short by some chaotic

madness of an impersonator
of importances who blindly
blandly robs another of
the yet to be experienced
inviting only scrapbooks
to be real for anyone to ponder

Seashells in the Seychelles

Trapeze moans beneath the swish
of gloam just farthings
from strung seashells
in the Seychelles

sand silver keynote plumbing
drained of ivy and perhapsness
as individual enlightenment
goes viral system to system

mono kissing like the washers
tucked between layers frothed
in nests of illumined spritz
of funds wanted and whatnot

pater nost- remaineth in coelis
as we whine from here short selling
jubilation thieved from books
on the reserved list painted in-depth blue

Seen On Screen

This patchwork of majestic syllables reverberates beneath silence,
a presumption carded at the door. Oh, not to be eighteen. The rim
shot and the miss, the overflow of dowager impediments. How gravy
washes down perceived normed substance. Nouns squeak their
depleted wheel light as they flash across the highway. Seen on screen
the rims move in reverse. Plush invariant recursion. As when flight, as
when immersion overtakes the butterfly.

Mores, feelgood chapparal, hope of cleanse and winter

III

whose guests we always are

It Is Trying to Fail to be a Monument

Ripeness is dimension seen through
bifocals you have to
let go awhile and wait
to learn what has learned you
according to a dialect denoting teach

I'm warning you I will not warn you
anymore I'm drying in the peach lit sun
I'm ornery as an adolescent grappling with gravity
a little pinkness surrounds my aspirations
until you remove what is
removable and give it back to where it goes again

Extrasensory emancipation yields to
The world as it has numbed us
In principio erat verbum
Clandestine as a pope and brisk
With proclamations others
Obviously require that they might prop up lives
Like fireflies in the corridor of summer
Near the breathless garden where bees
Beseech no one and spectators
Align with a tremolo fierce to freely framed
With silence equivalent to magic
And the magi double majoring
In op cit limelight forested

Four Autumn Ghazals

1/

Maternity requires no leave, merely biology.
She taps a pencil on the glass topped desk facing the window.

Metronomic capture of experience means invisible memories.
What is recorded lapses before it resurges to thought.

Velvety petals in a vivid purple taunt the soul
envisioning informal majesty at least for now.

A neighbor often is a mirror, and small talk, the polish.
Intervening variables make research harsh.

Listening perfumes interaction quietly.
A tipping point most often recognized in retrospect.

2/

She knows something by memory and cannot find the words.
How jostled recitation, given all things once considered.

Witnessing redeems theory from pretension.
Intaglio grows shrill to the point of no relief.

She routinely resides in the solarium.
Wildlife impinges on claimed centrality.

The thought of an infraction taints the myth of purity,
delicious as the mental faculties insist.

Research, best reported sung: soprano, alto, tenor, bass.
The conductor keeps making history in her tiny heart.

3/

Premonitions traipse across the landscape
of intention where the pale heart remembers.

Weather repeats the recent years untangling
a string of better living almost shared.

Clay like skin like firm protection holds its place
to keep sadness alive as part of the experience.

Corpus keepsake shines against the velvet
in the special box with polished wood.

The tenses look alike during meditation
as the sacrament of purity rinses itself.

4/

North of urban pastures lives a mountain made of salt.
She kismets afternoon by rote, primping probabilities.

A master stroke of genesis impedes the wild reversion
to encumber struts from breaking into newfound language.

Composition of the tree absorbs sufficient water
to deplete the lines of code made vocal as a tune.

Whispering repeals intention of emotion
drawn freehand and shared without a Rubicon.

How the water plays upon the light, reversing
quotients seen as real within rectangles arranged in flight.

My Sole Excuse

Others keep saying "Be

kind to yourself." I don't

know what that means.

All my life I have assigned

myself to do, to make,

and to produce what I believe

will outlast and thus transcend me,

now and at the hour.

I persist, I drive, I dream

of finished work I keep

producing, and I kneel to it

reflexively. That is my style,

my life, my sole

excuse for being.

Three Poems

~ 1 ~

I see a potshot in your future fungal rapture

Go ahead and preach to witless witnesses drowning

In unimpeachable arrears

The cat has left the catwalk integers have softened

To surprise versus blaspheme in expectation

One has come to long for amid unceasing patchwork

Of dribbled innocence maimed by foretaste

Of Mary Hails in pails of drop kick bloom lines

Penetrable as silk

We've wheezed along perimeters

Of sanctimonious pilfered slouch rinsed by blancmange

(Elsewhere *biancomangiare*)

Distinct from strophes of Senegal

My Sisyphus in retro paleo pronouncements

My Edith Hamilton my stonewall my impeccable alignment

With prom light dimmed to backseat pearls

Strung by village vox populi in traction

As the whetstone drives the yield

The blacklist of domain names

Hunched in alphabetical estrangement

Botulist as campsite V-formations

Trolloping across floorboards

~ 2 ~

She has no idea she has no idea

Within her psyche vein drops mitigate

The tempus fugue of dissonance

Framed then packaged then dispersed qua nurture

To inhabitants of curvy-lined locales

Lusting for hard sharp boundaries

To be claimed as owned replete with bones

That would preclude intrusion

As if petulant desire sufficed to shift identity

From safekeeping to pliable as defined

By minds seeking to self-bloat

Beneath whole clouds invis-appearing as if

To tame an otherwise flat blue sky

Unadorned by artists' nudges and kind eyes

Absorbing what is there or will be

Soon broken by advances into seasons left for bread

Crumbs to feed outliers who belong here

And whose guests we always are

~ 3 ~

You need a curfew need a flag to furl

You need a body hinged to mind-prone lickety hop

To spritz matchbook's historic staleness

Into fresh caught light to show

The podge hitched to the hodge within

Non-random lane lines veering toward a destination

That negates pathways while brandishing

Rigid thought as oxymoronic spree

Of damage control to sprawl the status quo

Suppressing fever frock in feathery pursuit

Of what might fill the empty space

As insects crawl across the warm spring screen

The familiar metaphor for what reality might seem

From faraway dimensions scattergrammed

As viaducts conjoined in a symphonic Braille of throughways

Pressuring advancement while cohabiting the known universe

In a companionable breeze of smooth predictive surfaces

With holes for breathing

As the act of breathing

Elevates to disappear

No Gravity

When he laughs, he hears the womanly inclusion of a crying sound,
afraid of letting go. There is no gravity to safen him. The monster boys
he wanted to touch or be are poised to show themselves. He has no
guarantee of something he can count on, he agrees to laugh, reveals
that he is willing to give in to what they want. He concedes points
never made, the rollerblade of envy that occupies some land he might
have owned. If only he could dwell unharmed and look across into
their eyes equal as thought.

14 Observations

Bureaucracy resists reasons for blood's hammering through veins.

#

When I think of her, I think of how much she has invested in comfort that is in fact uncomfortable because she constantly is reminded of how likely it is to go away.

#

Trees in the yard, so hushed and bountiful they do not need us.

#

Fences everywhere, most notably within the brain, so little light, so much light needed.

#

He marches well, his uniform fits faithfully, we require him, the cost of maintenance is high.

#

Birthdays make good markers, the quiver of sand meaning collectively something at any distance.

#

She drills down into her past to form a narrative that plays within the boundaries of others' sense of hearing.

#

Chance modesty arrives in tandem with a bouquet of adulation from out of nowhere, just when needed.

#

A pairing of reasons, rumored to be factually based, contages through the neighborhood, the town, the largest tract of land accessible.

#

He loses energy more rapidly than prayer evaporates from his psyche anymore, promoting retrospective digging in.

#

The screen she used when she was well enough to read and view is damaged now with food scars and repeated accidents.

#

Opulence lives on in the brain after so much formatting and insistence by collective memory, the salt on roadways eats away at crafted metal fins.

\#

Her speaking voice, soprano not surprisingly, moved deftly through
the content prompted by questions from a dinner companion randomly
assigned.

\#

Birds gather along the power lines perfect for sketches and
photographs from sufficient distance.

A Saturday

Good trees fat with fruit to pick and give away made sunlight
    worthwhile.

The to-do list took a nap in a low-hanging hammock the color mauve.

An herbal remedy to quash the guilt kicked in, to feed soul's softness.

A lorikeet ensconced in memory regaled those gathered to honor a
    pure life.

Low quotient of mispronunciation from elected officials and
    newscasters offered a shred of solace.

Fractions came loose from their purported whole to frame a glorious
    irreverence.

One person at a time spoke as if into a microphone pointed to angels.

A lifelike statue of a warm-blooded guide walked off the pedestal and
    hugged the throngs of pilgrims finding their way.

Ashwagandha

I want to bolt from the clandestine lust for a divinity within my scope.

I want to leeway into pastorals mid-city in the anchored garden of my
prior haste.

I want to taste the accidental flowers where they live and dry them for
the ages.

I want to reason with a nonexistent enemy fraught with silver and
suspension.

I want fenestration to reveal me to your druthers when I speak.

I want to obfuscate precisely zilch that we may hear each other over
every figurative fence.

I want to weasel out of consistency, as I revere the seasoned
imperfections.

I want amendments to your pretty constitution to align you with
eternity.

I want to empty out the granular inducements to underline an
otherwise rote message.

I want to climb into a television episode where two characters
    homogenize unlike ideas.

I want to dazzle off to a repetitive indulgence that transforms
    particulates into a wave of luster that defines who we will be.

I want to pour a rinse of evergreen over the voices blaming, naming
    names, confounding their environs.

I want the bleak beans to be pacified like candles reflexively perspiring
    gentle wax.

I want to simulate *pacem in terris* adverbially to emulsify desire and
    rest.

I want to integrate the free form staves inviting crafted instruments to
    their longevity.

A little Somersault

Rigamarole once
Stanched may
Blossom
A blouse
Size too
Toned bronze
My olive
Breath beside
Your homonymic
Leisure brash
Down calming
The pipe
Whose integer
Keeps smalling

Everything I Did

Everything I did, I did
to bring it home to you
and thank you for guiding me
toward what happened in a day.

Everything I did, we did,
back home each thing felt centered
from our centering together,
and came to mean what we let it mean.

Everything we did, I took into my heart
remembering verbatim each conversation,
and held also the unspoken, and released
the moments that just safely fell away.

Everything we did, I still hold in my heart.
Now I sit near you while you sleep.
I wait for you to wake that I might
feel you feel what I report.

Everything we did is still there.
The sequence of moments, how changed
we were repeatedly, how pure, and now
I recollect alone as you drift away.

Today

She introduces the topic of deer, speaks of their delicate ways, their
        grace,
and gentleness as they magically appear in the woods.

I begin to sing, "Home on the Range." She chimes in.
We savor and discuss the line, "And the skies are not cloudy all day."

Today is unseasonably warm in Arizona.
She thinks we are in Wyoming.
Her hospital bed rises and falls
as our twin voices chime

with an altitude that mirrors how free she almost is,
how much sadness I am learning to transcend.

The Rain

Though others claim to like the rain
As I hear soft droplets coming down
Gray fills my heart
Hope lifts and there seems no oasis

For a time my heart needs warmth
There is no center
Has the sky entirely faded now
The ladder of what seems possible falls

And I fall with it feeling
A particular quiet filling all around me
I look for sadness to be carried away
New flowers are a thought

I discover who I am in sunlight
The only light I can remember shifts
Away from what is here this moment
Joining the rain within me in my only heart

White Statue

"Grief is love with no place to go."
-        Louise Penny

White statue curled sideways lies in snow
Blank face of the sky reminisces heart
Once known, now orphaned in devotion
Silence turns a whisper lodged within the throat

Blank face of the sky reminisces heart
Tall walls repeat themselves
Silence turns a whisper lodged within the throat
Fire has crispened the loved body to fine ash

Tall walls repeat themselves
Enclosure safens skin to warm near whiteness
Fire has crispened the loved body to fine ash
Eyesight drifts into a keyhole, shifts the dark

Enclosure safens skin to warm near whiteness
Cold butterflies linger in the mind
Eyesight drifts into a keyhole, shifts the dark
A zither of touch prints holds still

Cold butterflies linger in the mind
A small window frames early speech
A zither of touch prints holds still
No compass ever pure enough to pinpoint love

A small window frames early speech
I have forgotten nothing of your voice
No compass ever pure enough to pinpoint love
Selves are only tentative

I have forgotten nothing of your voice
Leaves and limbs kiss chilled glass
Selves are only tentative
I learn my way through assumed infinity

Leaves and limbs kiss chilled glass
Stamina gloves tender skin
I learn my way through infinity
Lamentations fall to earth resisting light

Stamina gloves tender skin
Once known, now orphaned in devotion
Lamentations fall to earth resisting light
White statue curled sideways lies in snow

You Erased Penury and Wrote my Heart

Minutes hurt the small until we kiss them.
Where light falters, voice shallows in.

Poverty accepts its depth.
What shows is creased against a likelihood.

Fall windows into shoots we claim are new
to us and our intention. I read my heart to you.

I rinse my life, and I discover yours
as young as we project toward any wilderness.

Spring

I am the mother of the poem.
I watch her open her eyes
that teach my own
while deepening beyond
that first young tiny being.
I learn how young I am beside her.

I am the mother of her tiny heart
a miracle before my sight, my touch,
before my hearing breath and smell.
How is it the poem has found precision
in surprise and resemblance
to the blue wren drawn by Jeremy Boot?
How its flight affects tree light
and blossoms that fill the yard.

I am the mother of my own heart
listening to spring song among the tentative
small shoots pushing up through earth
to find a settled place that lifts freshness
to depth of feeling seeking language
that equates a soul to soul.

I am the mother of the poem's infinity,
as I conceive my own, the first eyes that I saw,
the overture of kindness at respectful distance
by the woman family legend says wore beige lace
to meet me for the first time.

Acknowledgments

The author is grateful to Jonathan Penton and Unlikely Books for selecting this gathering of poems for publication. Jonathan's insightful gift of engaging Tobey Hiller's editorial prowess enriched the process. Tobey's expertise and sensitivity were evident at every turn as she provided excellent suggestions for shaping and sharpening the book. Throughout the time of finalizing the manuscript, Tobey made this collaboration a joyful learning experience for me.

I also wish to thank the editors of the following journals for publishing individual poems: *Brave New World, First Literary Review East, Unlikely Stories Mark V, Offcourse, Bosphorous Review of Books, Where Is the River, Marsh Hawk Press, Abbey, The Sparrow's Trombone, Stride Magazine, Variety Pack, Ariel Chart International Literary Journal, Garfield Lake Review, Indefinite Space, Knot Magazine, Three Line Poetry, Backchannels, Clockwise Cat, above / ground press, Alternative Route, Literary Yard, New Croton Review, International Times, M58, Otoliths, New Croton Review, FELL SWOOP (SWOOPCARDS)* and *Rabble Review*.

Sheila E. Murphy's poetry appeared or is forthcoming in *Verse Daily, Lana Turner, Fortnightly Review, Poetry, Hanging Loose,* and others. Her recent book publications include *Escritoire* (Lavender Ink, 2025) and *Permission to Relax* (BlazeVOX Books, 2023). She was awarded the Gertrude Stein Poetry Award for *Letters to Unfinished J.* (Green Integer Press, 2003) and won the Hay(na)ku Book Prize for *Reporting Live From You Know Where* (Meritage Press, 2018). She lives in Phoenix, Arizona.

Other Books by Sheila E. Murphy

Escritoire. Lavender Ink. 2025.
Permission to Relax. BlazeVOX Books. 2023.
October Sequence 1-51. mOnocle-Lash Anti-Press. 2023.
Sostenuto. Luna Bisonte Prods. 2023.
Golden Milk. Luna Bisonte Prods. 2020.
As If to Tempt the Diatonic Marvel from the Ivory. Broken Sleep
    Books. 2018.
Reporting Live from You Know Where. Meritage Press / i.e. press and
    xPress(ed). 2018.
Underscore (with K.S. Ernst). Luna Bisonte Prods. 2018.
Ghazals 1-59 and Other Poems (with Michelle Greenblatt). Unlikely
    Books. 2017.
Yes It Is (with John M. Bennett). Luna Bisonte Prods. 2014.
2 Juries + 2 Storeys = 4 Stories Toujours (with K.S. Ernst). Xerolage
    55 from Xexoxial Editions. 2013.
Continuations 2 (with Douglas Barbour). The University of Alberta
    Press. 2012.
American Ghazals. Otoliths Press. 2012.
Noun that I've Been Watching. White Sky Books. 2012.
American Haibun. White Sky Ebooks. 2012.
The Daylight Sections. White Sky Books. 2011.
Beyond the Bother of Sunlight (with Lewis LaCook). BlazeVOX Books.
    2011.
Reverse Haibun. White Sky Books. 2011.
Circumsanct. White Sky Books. 2011.
Toccatas in the Key of D. Blue Lion Books. 2010.
This Is Visual Poetry. chapbookpublisher.com. 2010.

Quaternity (with Scott Glassman). Otoliths Press. 2009.
how to spell the sound of everything (with mIEKAL aND). Xerox Sutra
     Editions. 2009.
Reverse Haibun. Chalk Editions. 2009.
Circumsanct. Chalk Editions. 2009.
Collected Chapbooks. Blue Lion Books. 2008.
Parsings. Arrum Press (Finland). 2008.
Permutoria (with K.S. Ernst). Luna Bisonte Prods. 2008.
The Case of the Lost Objective Case. Otoliths Press. 2007.
Continuations (with Douglas Barbour). The University of Alberta Press.
     2006.
Incessant Seeds. Pavement Saw Press. 2005.
Proof of Silhouettes. Stride Press (UK). 2004.
Concentricity. Pleasure Boat Studio: A Literary Press. 2004.
Green Tea with Ginger. Potes & Poets Press. 2003.
Letters to Unfinished J. Green Integer Press. 2003.
The Stuttering of Wings. Stride Press (UK), 2002.
Heresiarch. Xtant Anabasis (VA), 2002.
Luminarias, Familiar Hinges. Wild Honey Press (Ireland), 2001.
The Indelible Occasion. Potes & Poets Press, 2000.
Numens From Centrality. Paper Brain Press (San Diego), 1999.
Leaflets. Instress (CA), 1998.
*Falling in Love Falling in Love With You Syntax: Selected and New
     Poems*. Potes & Poets Press, 1997.
A Little Syncopy. Marshall Creek Press (CA), 1996.
A Clove of Gender. Stride Press (UK), 1995.
A Brotherly Unfixed Grace-Noted Stare. Potes & Poets Press (CT),
     1995.
Pure Mental Breath. Gesture Press (Toronto), 1994.

Tommy and Neil. Sun/Gemini Press (Tucson, Arizona), 1993.
18/81. Gesture Press (Toronto), 1991.
Teth. Chax Press, 1991.
Sad Isn't the Color of the Dream. Stride Press (UK), 1991.
With House Silence. Stride Press (UK), 1987.
Virtuoso Bird Poems (with David Chorlton). Brushfire, 1982.
Fingers of Silence. Brushfire, 1981.

Recent Titles from Unlikely Books

Spells for the Wicked by Marc Vincenz
The Other Side of the Mirror: Excerpts and Additions to a Plantation Owner's Diary by Aileen Bassis
Dora/Lora by Larissa Shmailo
Here, Which Is Also a Place by Mark DuCharme
Handling Filth: Simple Sabotage Field Manual by Jared Schickling
White Van by Meg Tuite
Flight Advice by Tobey Hiller
A Brief Conversation with Consciousness by Marc Vincenz
~getting away with everything by Vincent A. Cellucci and Christopher Shipman
fata morgana by Joel Chace
Typescenes by Rodney A. Brown
Political AF: A Rage Collection by Tara Campbell
The Deepest Part of Dark by Anne Elezabeth Pluto
Swimming Home by Kayla Rodney
Manything by dan raphael
Citizen Relent by Jeff Weddle
The Mercy of Traffic by Wendy Taylor Carlisle
Cantos Poesia by David E. Matthews
Left Hand Dharma: New and Selected Poems by Belinda Subraman
Apocalyptics by C. Derick Varn
Pachuco Skull with Sombrero: Los Angeles, 1970 by Lawrence Welsh
Monolith by Anne McMillen
When Red Blood Cells Leak by Anne McMillen
anonymous gun. by Kurtice Kucheman
Soy solo palabras but wish to be a city with words by León De la Rosa and illustrations by Gui.ra.ga7